Face Half-Illuminated

"These are luminous writings. They touch on memory and presence, they bridge cultures and generations, they point always toward our shared blessings. The powerful and well-crafted works in this collection show the fruits of a life lived fully, attentively and gratefully. How delightful to discover a publisher and a book that embrace several genres under the same cover so that an author's work can explore many facets of human expression. The final essay on translation is perhaps one of the most important and insightful essays written on that subject and will serve well both translators and those who read works in translation."

—Michael Glaser, Poet Laureate of Maryland, 2004-2009

"Danuta E. Kosk-Kosicka's writing is irresistibly irresistible. At once a biochemist and a poet, at once Polish and American, at once dreaming of the past and living in the present, she offers us her own poems and translations of poems written by her mother, the Polish poet Lidia Kosk, that hook us immediately. Whether Ms. Kosk-Kosicka is writing about what happened in Poland during World War II or what's happening on the Beltway, whether she's speaking of her love for translating or the beautiful dance of the globes in a city square in Mexico, she speaks with a lush precision and love of words that draws us into her world."

—John Z. Guzlowski, Author of *Lightning and Ashes*

"What these poems of mother and daughter share: their sensory aliveness, a vision illuminated by beauty and darkened by war, and painful longing for a childhood home and a world at peace.

'In Your Voice My Name,' my favorite of Danuta's translations, is a deceptively simple lullaby of longing in which mother and daughter are one infant, safe for a moment in the memory of a mother's voice."

—Mary Azrael, Poet and Editor of *Passager*

"In 1980 a young scientist comes to America from Poland—from behind the Iron Curtain. Today, this poet lives among us, and translates poems to hold fast to her life and those of her loved ones. Danuta E. Kosk-Kosicka sets out to recapture the iconography of her life here, and in Poland. She writes her poems in English, also translating her mother's work in a compelling range of poems. This is a personal and historical conversation, through imagery and cadence, communicating memories and beliefs. There's a strong will at the center of each poem that, with the benefit of translation, affords new versions of existing poems. Translating is a beautiful obsession, and this poet speaks of her achievements in an essay that makes her unique artistry legible. She proves to us in prose and verse that, with a rich heart, anything is possible."

—Grace Cavalieri, Poet and Producer of *"The Poet and the Poem from the Library of Congress"*

"The 'face half-illuminated' to which the title of this book alludes is that of a Polish poet and scientist who has embraced the light and promise of a new country without ever relinquishing the past and the shadow cast over it by the Nazi occupation of Poland. Danuta E. Kosk-Kosicka embodies that which she most desires, 'the power to expand this hour.' She revisits her youth and young womanhood in Poland and, beyond that, the preceding generation, as revealed in her translations of poems by her mother, the poet Lidia Kosk. Propelled by the need to retrieve the 'knapsack of memories' left behind by those who did not survive this turbulent period in Polish history, mother and daughter join voices in this luminous collection of poems and essays—a must read for anyone who either knows or wants to understand what it means to live in two worlds."

—Sue Ellen Thompson, Poet and winner of the 2010 Maryland Author Award

Acknowledgments

I want to extend my heartfelt thanks to these special people who read *Face Half-Illuminated* in whole or in part, and offered invaluable feedback: Shirley J. Brewer, Kathleen Corcoran, Andrzej J. Kosicki, Piotr H. Kosicki and Margaret S. Mullins.

❖

Grateful acknowledgment is made to the following publications in which the following works first appeared, sometimes in a different form:

Poems by Danuta E. Kosk-Kosicka
"Face Half-Illuminated, Half in Shadow," *Pirene's Fountain*
"My Mother at Twelve," *International Poetry Review*
"Lilac Lilacs," *Passager*
"Now, When I Can See," *The Gunpowder Review*
"Coffee with Carya," *Pivot*
"Once She is Here We Will," *Loch Raven Review*
"That Line in the Protocol," *Möbius, The Poetry Magazine*
"In and Out of the Jungle," *Stranger At Home, An Anthology: American Poetry With An Accent*
"Driving on the Beltway," *Weavings 2000: The Maryland Millennial Anthology*
"Holiday Morning in the Tatra Mountains," with the title, "Holiday Morning in Zakopane," *Thy Mother's Glass*

"Morelia: Dance of the Globes," *Stranger At Home, An Anthology: American Poetry With An Accent*

"My Mother at Twelve" appears in *Oblige the Light,* the winner of the fifth annual Clarinda Harriss Poetry Prize (CityLit).

Essays by Danuta E. Kosk-Kosicka
"Turning to Poetry," as "Why I turned to poetry:" On Being Invisible: Foreign Authors, *Little Patuxent Review*
"A Note on Translating," *Loch Raven Review*

Poems by Lidia Kosk, translated by Danuta E. Kosk-Kosicka
"The Blacksmith's Daughter," *One Tree, Many Branches*
"In the Current of the River," *International Poetry Review*
"Our Children," *Contemporary Writers of Poland*
"And I See Those Streets," *Loch Raven Review*
"Calvados," *The Dirty Goat*
"From Afar," *Against Agamemnon: War Poetry 2009*
"Before a Human Killed With a Human," *September Eleven: Maryland Voices Anthology.*
"In Your Voice My Name," *The Dirty Goat*

Except for "In the Current of the River" and "And I See Those Streets," all other translations appeared in Lidia Kosk's two bilingual books: *niedosyt/reshapings* and *Słodka woda, słona woda/Sweet Water, Salt Water.*

"From the Window of My Apartment" and "Obligations" are now newly composed works set for mixed choir by Philip A. Olsen and have been performed in the USA and Peru. Both have been translated into multimedia video productions by Ryan Sevel.

To the amazing Lidia Kosk, my mother

Contents

Turning to Poetry

❖

I arrived in the USA on June 30, 1980, right after receiving my Ph.D. in biochemistry from the Polish Academy of Sciences. A couple of months later, the Polish trade union Solidarity (Solidarność) was born. As a result, the Polish government allowed my husband to join me in the States in December.

My first trip to a Safeway in San Francisco was a shock: overstocked shelves in long aisles, so many kinds of everything. Countless varieties of cooking oil and salad dressing from which to choose—and five-pound bags of sugar—at a time when, in Poland, stores were empty and food was rationed. Then and there, I decided that I didn't need sugar in my tea.

At that time, I was a rare specimen from behind the Iron Curtain: a scientist with a postdoctoral fellowship. People seemed really interested in life in that Communist country even if they were not sure where Poland was. They asked me questions; they talked to me. There was so much to learn about our different worlds. They were learning from me, while I was learning from them about the United States.

When my fellowship ended two years later, Solidarity's leadership was behind bars, with martial law imposed in Poland. Flights were canceled, phone lines dead. My plane ticket home for Christmas 1981 went to waste. Later, when mail and phone connections resumed they were censored and unreliable. My husband and I stayed here. I was awarded my own research grants. Our son was born. I had a busy and successful career as an associate professor at Johns Hopkins University and also at the University of Maryland at Baltimore until I couldn't work anymore due to fibromyalgia.

Why did I turn to poetry?

In 1980, Czesław Miłosz was awarded the Nobel Prize in Literature. He was right in our backyard, a professor at Berkeley. My fellow researchers were amazed: Miłosz, a poet from Poland. In 1996, Wisława Szymborska was awarded the same prize. By then in Baltimore, I faced questions about this other Polish poet. Since Szymborska's books were not available in English, I translated one of her poems for a friend. I was thrilled by the journey from one language to another. It spurred me on to translating poems written by Lidia Kosk, my mother, the author of several books. While reading and re-reading her poems in the process of translating them, I relived some of her experiences—as well as my remembrance of them—and learned about others.

As was typical in my parents' generation, Lidia Kosk came of age during World War II and survived first the Nazi occupation of Poland and then the Stalinist regime imposed on Poland by the Soviet Union. As a young girl, she was twice captured by Nazis in random round-ups of Polish citizens that frequently led to death in German concentration camps. She escaped both times. Despite what she went through, she still believes that human beings are inherently good, even though there is a part of us that is evil and can be activated by ideology. These experiences have surfaced in her poems and short stories.

Over the years, I went on translating other Polish poets, including Ernest Bryll, author of countless volumes of poetry, plays, and prose. I have also translated poems by three Maryland Poets Laureate—Lucille Clifton, Josephine Jacobsen, and Linda Pastan—into Polish for publication in Poland. Life in two languages in the two countries has allowed me the unique opportunity to translate poetry and to form a bridge between the distinctive worlds and cultures defined by those languages.

At the same time, my own poems started appearing in English. From the back of the recycled pages of drafts of my biochemistry and biophysics manuscripts, they—gradually, slowly— earned their own sheets of paper.

Cut off from my family and country by martial law, I intensely missed them. The emotions, the dreams, geographical distance, isolation, and ultimately my fibromyalgia all came to the surface in the form of words and images. Sometimes, when a poem could not decide in which language it wanted to be written, I painted it with acrylics.

I have lived in two languages and written in both. The first poem in this collection, from which I drew the title for the book—"Face Half-Illuminated, Half in Shadow"—was born on an airplane, on the return flight from a family visit to Warsaw. I started writing it in Polish shortly after take-off. Then, somewhere over the Atlantic, I switched to English.

That was 1997, 15 years after martial law. Travel to Poland was no longer just a dream, especially after the Polish parliamentary elections of June 1989, which resulted in the appointment of Central and Eastern Europe's first non-Communist prime minister since World War II.

My mother has visited the USA several times. In 2003, she came following the publication of the bilingual *niedosyt/reshapings*, and we had the incredible experience of presenting the book together in two languages at a variety of venues, including Baltimore's Enoch Pratt Free Library, the Polish National Alliance, McDaniel College in Westminster, and the Polish Embassy in Washington. She recited her verse in Polish, and I read my English renditions.

When I read my poems, I usually include my translations of other poets, accompanied by the Polish originals. I also provide information on Polish history, literature, and the poet in question. I see it as my mission as a poet to foster an appreciation of history and other cultures. While presenting Lidia Kosk's war poems, I have noticed that people appreciate hearing that World War II started in Europe on September 1, 1939 with the invasion of Poland. Afterward, somebody usually comes forward to confess that he or she is of Polish descent but does not speak the language. Or knows just a few words, like my friend, who learned from her grandmother, *Babcia*, who did not know much English. At the beginning of the 20th century, it was still believed that speaking another language at home hampered one's education and chances of success in America.

While assembling the book, I made choices. From among hundreds of poems, I picked the ones that speak to and complement each other. For example, I offer readers who turn to Lidia's poems the opportunity to recognize the place in the countryside that enchanted me when I first visited as a child. She lovingly introduced me to the linden tree that she had entrusted with her childhood secrets, and to the house on the hilltop, the place where she grew up a generation earlier under very difficult circumstances. I loved to visit there on carefree vacations. It is in my poems written in the USA that I return to the places and people with whom I have formed magical bonds.

Poems by Danuta E. Kosk-Kosicka

❖

Face Half-Illuminated, Half in Shadow

*

Beyond the small window a woolly sheet
underneath a dark gray wing. Isolated,
we turn our clocks back—at first
cautiously, just one hour. Of world's colors
only gray, blue, and white remain.
We drink over our losses,
stuff the emptiness with meals.
When we bravely turn our clocks back again
the smaller clouds blush. We begin to believe
our powers over time. But at 2 pm above the white
blinding vastness the moon
turns up. Below, the mountains rise,
icefields crack.

**

Tea time: a scone with clotted cream.
I unpack the spoon—mounds
of heavy cream frosting float by.
Needles on my window pane
spell: b e w a r e.

***

One more hour left. The passengers debate
whether it's 6 am or 6 pm. In Warsaw
concealed by heaven
my parents sleep
at twelve am. On I-95 in Maryland
at 6 pm my husband and son are nearing
the place where I will touch the earth.

My Mother at Twelve
Minkowice, Poland, 1940

Hours of waiting at the bakery,
all my money for a last loaf of bread.
Now, cycling kilometers to hunger at home.

Near the hamlet where roads cross,
I see German soldiers rounding up people,
my friend Hana among them.

I jump off the bicycle, run toward Hana
with the still-warm bread. "Death for helping Jews,"
the soldier points his gun at my chest. I trip and fall;
a bullet wails.

When darkness lifts,
I see trampled bread on the empty road.

Dream in a Red Coat

1.
They knock at a door. Steps approach,
a woman opens, slowly.
Oh, look at the tiny wild strawberry.
Come in,
since you are here.

2.
A young cavalry soldier: uniform, *rogatywka* cap,
smooth, narrow chin, aquiline nose, sharp eyes—
my father's, in that photograph. Green water
rises half-way to the horse's sides.

3.
In the serrated, black & white miniature
my sister stands between my parents
on a Baltic sea pier: chubby face,
a bow in her light-filled locks.
No, that's me.

4.
I dream-think: mother with her child
looks for a hiding place, girl in the red coat.
And again, my father on the horse, and water
soundless, soft.

5.
What do I know, what can I do?
I can connect with the moment
when my parents lift up the receiver
of the telephone on a distant ocean
shore in a different time zone.

Lilac Lilacs

A big branch of lilac. Lilac.
Like the ones along the village road.
The carriage wheels through the sand,
yellow splashes of warblers whir
through the fragrance. Lilac smells
like…lilac—May in Poland, warm days,
evenings not willing to sleep, simmering
desires. And then the verses
sound, better than any before. I can't open
my eyes to write them down. So I repeat
them over and over and slip
into another dream. I am gliding
through the air of music
toward luminous mountains.
I see myself as Chagall's
figure, long hair floating
parallel to my long dress. An orchestra
plays Elgar's "In the South"
and for the whole time I am there,
and the mountains, and the light.
Then a phone rings and I wake up
to answer, but the phone
does not ring. The birds
sing into my room. I come
down and can't find that poem.
But the lilacs,
the lilac lilacs…

Danuta E. Kosk-Kosicka

Now, When I Can See

Now, when
the rain curtain is up
a ray from over the hill
shoots its way through my window.

Soon the doors will sound
their evening routine;
then the dark screens will drop,
summoning evening chores.

Give me the power
to expand this hour; watch
over my fingers holding the pen
moving in the red glow.

Coffee with Carya

With the first dip of biscotti came the memory
of the walnut tree. How did I get to it? On the outskirts

of the orchard, behind the well, at the side of the house.
Round, green, tough skin, hulls, palms browned before the mouth
got the bittersweet seeds. Grandma would bring them when she arrived
right before the Christmas tree and the first star. Awaited
in the breathing of fir needles, waxed floor, poppy seed noodles,
tangerines. After the *Wigilia* Supper, singing the carols
was like being in church, flowers on woolen Sunday shawls
rose with high voices, and eyes flamed from candles.
The blue-robed statuette of Mary smiled.
So, how did I get there?

From the train I see her wait. The horses pace
their way between fields ripe with smells and huts
whitened for me. Hollyhocks against the scrubbed walls,
red begonia windows. The town churchyard
where Grandpa and Great-Grandma lie.
Wio, wio; when I wake up we have turned into the avenue
that before the war belonged to a *dwór*.

I jump down from the straw-filled seat between four boards,
greet the lined-up mulberry trees, and dye my hands with
the taste of white and dark berries. Kick off my shoes and feel the soil,
the sand when the carriage makes a left between bending grains'
warm hush and buckwheat's honeyed hum. I stop to pick
red poppies and ruffled blue cornflowers,
later to make cornflower wine with Grandma. I recognize
neighbors' farms hidden in groves.

And now it comes: The shiny roof of the blacksmith's shop,
thatched stables, two silver firs. I run on the nicest
carpet of greens that straighten up after the touch of feet,
hooves and wheels. To the house with the well and fruit trees,
like an altar, above the world down there—across the hay
grass and the talking stream—
where the sun used to retreat so the cows and horses
would return home and the frogs would sing.

Warm Stone, Cold Water

Apples daydream under parent trees.
Red raspberries glow by the side window.
Pears land softly in the grass; bees
dance on their bruised blushing skins.
A chestnut horse drinks from the trough
beside the well—
      a pail waits on the stone ledge.
Touching the stone, I look into the well's depth,
see myself chanting words.

Once she is here we will

drink thick sweet coffee from small cups
imprinted with diamonds, hearts,
clubs, and spades that bring back the taste
of bridge-playing on the porch, sand grains
sifting from sunbathed hair and toes
flip-flopped back from the beach;

pick out beads to restring
old necklaces, amber and coral silence,
remembering
our morning finds of glimmers in the seaweed
brought ashore by high tide—
sun beams sinking, passing through the current;

arrange years of photographs
which she missed,
see her grandson the first time he
met the ocean's weave and roar—his feet
gliding over the mirrored shore
his arms up toward the sea;

drive to the coast, let go our shoes,
imprint our soles—
left, right, hers larger than mine,
parallel, diffused where the sand is hot and dry,
deep and clear toward the water line—
dig in to watch a seagull, a sailboat, a wave
pick up a shell;

perhaps
next time, perhaps,

for now she is on the plane
back through time zones
earthskyocean
in minute panes
leaving.

Detour from Obligations

Navigating among the established
and the freshly carved, still-steaming obligations

I escape outdoors
through yesterday's glaciers
softening to white comforters.

On a honeycomb path imprinted by wheelers
I reach the side-street loop.
A garbage truck roars and gulps refuse containers,
people's used and unused baggage.
The chomping sound

finds me gazing into the past
painted on the hill with the red barn
on the other side of the stream
where seven horses
molded from three colors of clay
straighten up as if listening.

Christmas trees still wait at the curb for their mulching trip.

I return to the interiors roamed by demands
that in my absence lost their edges.

That Line in the Protocol

"Cut the brain into small pieces..." The glass pane
of a huge window cuts me away from the metropolis below,
bloodied by Halloween's sunset.

Dressed in my white lab coat, I know that the line means
a prelude to an experiment, entrance to a labyrinth
of substructures, enzymes, neurotransmitters, nanomolecules.

Yet with the glare of eerie light rising and dying in the sky,
I see the rat brain transform into a daily
morning-noon-afternoon-night human mind—
a scientist-poet-woman-mother-wife.

As the chilly blackness steals the splendid sky,
the poet shocks the scientist by likening the mind
to grandma's pin cushion, densely pierced.
More and more pins pushed in.

In and Out of the Jungle

Boredom in the jungle, days on end,
seeps in from leaves green *ad nauseam.*
Cut off from light imprisoned above, my thoughts
rust in the dampness. The guerrillas clean their guns,
laugh, play cards, drowse.

Cockroaches in the jungle, days on end;
before I go to wash, the guerrillas
check for them, understanding my fear.
But once, soap-covered, I ran out
haunted by the flying beasts.

The Leader in his jungle stronghold
looks straight at me, his gun points at my heart,
you see two bodyguards at his side, more were there;
I took this photograph for "Time."
       Then he gave me his gun to admire;
the thought like a live wire
bolted through my mind: "Would I?"

Time for my job comes without warning;
jump in the jeep, full speed out of the jungle
we go to shoot. I follow their footsteps
swiftly, bodies on the ground
I catch in best light, full color.
       I give them immortality—
tomorrow for everyone to see
the still, bloodied villagers will scream
from glossy magazines, beyond the reach of fear.

Dizzy Spring

The house aches
in the morning brightness
fights for breath
frightened gray
vinyl skin shivers

in the wind
nagging
like a child at her mother's
                    long woolen coat
out there at the door
both determined and lost
they stand next to the crocuses

that try hard over and over—bold
velvet purple, boiling yellow, shy
white—none lucky or strong
enough to bloom longer than it takes to sprout
through the layers of ground
half-frozen, half-mud

over and over in the Spring's brightness
blooming, white, frozen, yellow, gloomy, mud,
wind, dizzy, frightened, struggling, mother, child.

Driving on the Beltway

I miss the earthliness.
Instead of the buoyant
steadiness of forsythia's yellow,
expectancy of apple tree buds

breathing their white insides
open in fragrance,
the coolness of tulip leaves
slowly unwrapping in wisps of laughter,

I feel the push of passing cars,
the uneven pavement,
borders of broken lines,
concrete barriers. While I count

the exits, the minutes crawl
along my spine,
deposit lead in my thighs.
I long for a whiff of chocolate mulch

freshly piled around the trees.
To stop.
To touch the porous skin.
To be touched.

Holiday Morning in the Tatra Mountains

for my mother

In the fog that engulfs our manor at the creek
we forgive ourselves the sin of insatiability
we forgive ourselves for today
all unaccomplished deeds

and looking at the drops
hung on the terrace
for birds and brook to perform
before the altar of Giewont

dozing behind the clouds
in the softness of morning discourse—tolling bells,
bathing pots, bellowing dogs—we engulf
ourselves in a sleep without dreams.

Morelia: Dance of the Globes

The towers have separated from the naves
and sing with the bells, leaving
the blue-tiled dome in the earthly domain
with people on the plaza

lit only here and there by retreating sun:
golden spikes on the gates, bubbling fountain
sprays. People take over sun-warmed
walls, benches, pavement stones.

To the left a boy reclines with his wares
filled with soap-bubble water. To the right

a girl dances among globes of light;
her heavy boots, her whirling skirt,
her hands extend to the glowing spheres.
Her father laughs and blows more soap

bubbles. A toddler wobbles in the swirl of balls
that whisper, twinkle, promise, and go.

I wish I could stay,
watch this picture on the square.
But the towers have rejoined the cathedral,
all the spheres are joining the blue shadow,

and I have to leave this time and place
with the feeling of slow-motion happiness
of a small town *skwer* in long ago
Poland on a sunny Sunday.

Poetry Dialogue—*szansa*

"Dialogue Among Civilizations"
is on.
Names. Faces.
My face next to the microphone.
My mother's name—
I am reading her poem.
One, two…at the count of five
the words come:

"A Chance.

To live
I need, like air,
human kindness…"

I translate her words, try their English
counterparts for feelings, hues, sounds,

move them across the page,
across the ocean.

In my poems I go to the USA,
Mexico, Sri Lanka, Poland.

A girl dancing in a swirl of globes,
I am tasting her verses, and mine,

in the tongue she gave me,
in the space of a chance—*szansa.*

Poems by Lidia Kosk
Translated by Danuta E. Kosk-Kosicka

❖

The Blacksmith's Daughter

The twinkling little stars of her childhood sprang
from the burning-hot iron
hammered by her father into
horseshoes. Not for good luck
but for protection of horses' hooves

She kept the fire burning—
bellows and quickened breath—
she hardened like a red-hot
horseshoe plunged into water

She kept for life the iron strength
and the longing for gentleness

In the Current of the River

Let's assume that the river continues to flow
among the swaying grasses, interspersed
by small mirrors of water and young alders
still growing

full of vortices, self-cleaning
fordable where the bottom
is hardened by gravel. Across such
spots we ran from the Germans

Grandma, preparing our meager supper, saves a slice of bread
crosses herself, glances at the door, wondering if
the ones needing help will appear quietly out of the shadows
or the others, the armed ones, will break in

the puppy's head pokes out from under a threadbare blanket
eyes closed—tonight we are safe. In the morning the Germans shoot
30 Poles. The next day, the Poles will fire at
the German military train, which rolls with the war

People will not return to their homes, the river
will flow, the alders will grow and hide the bodies

Birth of the World
for Danusia

Chubby miniature
scented like a child
running between bird and earth
like the sun catching with radiant fingers
the white house on the hilltop, whose
slopes glisten in the morning dew
and breathe thyme of midday air

emerging from the horizon of gestures
molecules of you and me
with eyes like heaven before the rebellion of angels
announces another birth of the world

Our Children

When they started hearing, they heard
guns and bullets rattle
in the stories
about the invasion, about the war

When they started seeing, they saw
people being killed
in the stories
about the invasion, about the war

They were born to peace time
but in their parents' eyes,
like on a movie reel, the war
rolled on

And we, the parents, rejoiced
that our children had been spared the war

Danuta E. Kosk-Kosicka

And I See Those Streets

Lublin, Poland
much younger
gloomier
yet so close

I wander
along the main street of my city
crammed with people and buildings
clinging to the pavement
I step back into the churches
that embrace the passersby—
Capuchins', St. Joseph's
Visitandines', Holy Spirit—
teeming with navy blue-and-white uniforms
I see myself kneel on the stone steps
of the main altar to ask for
the grace of freedom, bread, wisdom
and good fortune for my loved ones
Through the open door
I hear the crash of Nazi military boots
hard like the gaze of their masters

I pause on the city square
which, like a key ring
binds the Royal, Hircine
Holy Spirit and New-Lubartów streets
to Krakowskie Street
before delivering them to the arc
of the Krakowska Gate
to guard, and to protect

My defenseless memory brings back the screams—

I am caught in a roundup
On the pavement
boots, boots, military boots
overpowering shouts, beating, yanking
ramming into the backs of trucks
stunned random victims
who will be sent to labor and concentration camps

From the truck
moving along Krakowskie Street
a girl jumps out into the crowd

A whir of a bullet—Cut

Memory's film moves forward
Scenes from Chopin Street overlap:
Silence soaks the pain of a dying young man
kicked to a pulp on the pavement
by boots, boots, military boots
which stepped over our eastern border
Screams of another tortured victim
jumping from the window of the interrogation room
envelop the petrified mother
His body freed by death
will not be honored by the funeral march

I hear the memory of the street

Now facing the Krakowska Gate I am safe
but the strikes of each hour
throb with the terrors of that war
wounding the memory of my city

Flower in Your Hair

My city—
　　　　so sad today
with faces of people
　　　　who follow
the disfigured reflections
　　　　of intents
Girl—
　　　　May-girl
so good that you have
　　　　pinned a flower in your hair
for a rendezvous
　　　　with your May paramour
in the romantic
　　　　spring forest
He will
　　　　return with you
back to the city
　　　　unlike the grandfathers
who had to hide
　　　　in the forest
Their faces veiled
　　　　in failed choices
chiseled in stone
　　　　time dusted
bestow
　　　　sadness on the streets
Streets of my city—
　　　　change!
Girl—so good
　　　　that you have
a flower in your hair

Obligations

You are running
Constantly
In a hurry
Performing thousands of tasks
No time
For yourself
But it doesn't matter
You are judged
By your obligations to others
You didn't make it
You couldn't
You explain
Then there is blame
You have
No right to stop
You keep running
In a hurry
Touched by love
Bits of tenderness
Obligations!
Your marathon
Without a finish
Without fanfares
Still running

Danuta E. Kosk-Kosicka

From the Window of My Apartment

Above the apartment house
whose windows exchange looks with mine
the moon got stuck
among the rocks and boulders of clouds
He kept hanging there, stubbornly
until I forgot that I had broken with him
permanently
Until I forgot that my soul
did not sing anymore
Until all of me was a song

At the Bottom of the White Canyon

I am a dot at the bottom
of an upside-down
vanilla ice-cream cone
Up there, so far above
a drop of sky
I am. I am alive

Does my being affect the stones
and walls of piled-up white?
Numbing nothingness

I am saved only
by my thirst for the blue sky

Baltimore, Farewell

for Andrzej

Again I am saying farewell to my harbor
vibrating
in the heat-wave fever
flooded with lights

Flickering
on the film of water
skyscrapers
and wild ducks
bound to the concrete
by the magnet of night

The ship is leaving

Calvados
for Piotr

I sip calvados instilled
with a whisper of Remarque's pen
dark current of the Seine
chill of cloud drifts
surrounding our plane

Blissfully fatigued after the conquest
I float over Arc de Triomphe
once again
find Chopin at Père Lachaise
in Luxemburg Gardens hold a monologue
with the stone lion
soar into Pantheon's firmament captured in my lens
until scratched by a spike on the tower
I fall on the bridge by Notre Dame

In the droplets of the spirit
like a snake
dances the desire
to encounter Paris
on all the bridges of his Seine

Memoirs after the Cities

In the most splendid
cities of the world
there is at least one
gray roof
sad and lonely
as a man could be

So easy so hard to look away

In the small unsightly
cities of the world
there is at least one
sunny roof
cheerful and radiant
as a man could be

Golden Gate Bridge
sends its lustrous reds
to the roofs of San Francisco
Eyes of the Skylon Tower
reflect city roofs
shimmering in crystal
drops of Niagara Falls

On the chessboard
of Old Town roofs
mystery lights caught
from the Royal Column
by the Warsaw moon move
waiting for the sun

My eyes see
tops
of rosy houses
and green trees
I want to stay
happy just a bit longer

From Afar

the surface of the Baltic seems smooth

the time and space wedged between us
do not stop me from looking for you

you fought for this town
you fought for this coast

I can't see weapons in your hands
I can't see your hands at all
I see the deep of your eyes

you wore no glasses then
just your twenty years
on the front line

a breaking wave
brings back bits of that time
your eyes full of young hope

I must recover your knapsack
of memories

Before a Human Killed With a Human

Spills of redness saturated
bandages of clouds
and paled uncovering
a big shield of Sun
The brightness captured our plane

Suddenly it waned
hid behind the falling wall
of indigo clouds driven in
by the last ray
Silent moment of darkness fell

We crossed the threshold
Gold-saturated shimmering dawn
dissolved uncovering
the big shield of Sun
It permeated the windows of the plane

The dream that didn't make it
slipped down the ball of Earth
between the red and the gold
of sunset and sunrise
A new ordinary day was born

before a human killed with a human
planes and buildings
full of humans

Danuta E. Kosk-Kosicka

In Your Voice My Name

When the little I
wrapped in a blanket
whimpered in disquiet
you called to me
and cradled me
in your smile

The sound of my name
in the safety of your voice
unlocked the worlds

Your voice
like a sliver of childhood
stays with me

Mother, call me
call my name often

Before even the longest trip
upon hearing your voice
I will dutifully answer
I am coming

A Chance

To live
I need, like air
human kindness
space
color and fragrance of the world

I run away from
jarring noise
mustiness
damaging anger

As long as there is a place for my return
I have a chance

A Note on Translating

❖

When the Polish poet Wisława Szymborska won the Nobel Prize for Literature in 1996, and my American friends started asking about her writings, I set out to translate into English one of her poems for my friend Alice, whose grandparents had emigrated from Poland in the 19th Century. I chose "The People on the Bridge." I enjoyed flowing through the seemingly peaceful poem, then almost shuddering at its ending. I had at least two ideas on how to translate the last sentence of the poem. So I gathered some friends who were native Polish speakers and asked for their takes on the ending; we came up with four versions. Obviously, I needed to ponder all the possibilities and make a decision. I imagined being a director staging a play. I thought of all the different interpretations of Hamlet that I had seen.

Soon, two different books of Szymborska translations were out, and Alice was excited to find "her" poem included in both. "Each translation is different from yours and from the others," she mused. We set out to compare them. We looked for the best lines that, according to us, would create the best version. I realized that, while there may never be a perfect translation, the translating process is exciting and challenging.

I was still hesitant to translate. I started by choosing poems from Lidia Kosk's books that I thought would easily lend themselves to the English language. I didn't fully realize all the possible problems. So much so that I began with a rhyming poem! When my translation was later published in the literary journal *Passager*, I was hooked. I have continued translating my mother's poems at a slow pace; once we had made the decision to publish a bilingual book, the pace accelerated. The book came out in 2003. The biggest challenge was its title; the Polish *niedosyt* is a word of multiple meanings, which after weeks of torture I decided to "change" to *reshapings*. The poet agreed to that change. For her second bilingual book, with the practice gained over years, I translated all her new poems as they came to me via the Internet.

Translating the work of a poet who is available for consultation is a great advantage when questions arise. For example, am I allowed to change personal names so that they are easy to pronounce in the other language, or so that the sound fits the poem in a comparable way to the original? What if the name has a special meaning to the author? I posed such a question to Lucille Clifton while translating into Polish her poems "praise song" and "moonchild." I appreciated the opportunity to ask Linda Pastan whether the children in her poem "Ethics" were girls, as in the Polish language the verb forms are different depending on the person's gender. I was also fortunate enough to be able to discuss with Josephine Jacobsen her poem "Last Will and Testament" for the Polish translation. The consultations encouraged me to continue.

In the course of studying various approaches to translating poetry I have become more aware of linguistic and poetic traps and the choices to be made. For example, is it better to be a literal or a liberal translator? I have discovered that some translators don't know the language from which they translate. Apparently, they get a rough translation from someone else, or rely on a translation into another language they know; then, they exercise the poet's magic to create a poem in English. Or they rely on some earlier renditions into English to work out their own. The other extreme might be a word-for-word translation. But what if a word has two or even more meanings? What if this creation in the new language has the same meaning but a different tone and form? What if it has lost its inherent magic?

Translating poetry is both a creative process and detective work of sorts. It's always a learning experience. When I translate a poem, I read it many times and usually discover something new. There's the structure, the rhythm, the key words, the special effects, the layers of meaning, the diction, the mood created, and the words or phrases with double meanings that lack their counterparts in the other language. It struck a chord when I heard that the Swedish translator of Szymborska's work, Anders Bodegård, had said that he would not even attempt translating some of her poems, as the play on words could not be translated into his language.

I often return to a translation still pondering whether I got it right. Reading, thinking it over, sounding it out—these are the stages in the work of transforming the poem from one language into another, be it from English to Polish, or from Polish to English, as has been my experience. I wasn't scared to start translating between languages; luckily, I was not aware at the time that translators in the USA usually translate only into English.

I know of people who learn a language so that they can read their favorite poets in the original. The second-best option is to compare various renderings of the same poem by different translators to get a better feel for the possible nuances. The most famous poets have many translators, and with practice it becomes possible to recognize the author of a given translation. By rendering a poem in the new language the translator leaves an imprint by transforming it according to the requirements of the language as well as translator's knowledge and sensitivity.

As a translator, does it help to be a poet? A panel of four translators, which I had the privilege to moderate, provided a whole range of responses to the question from the audience. There is no one "right" answer. I believe that it helps, especially when the two parties share a similar poetic sensitivity. Most of all, it helps tremendously, whether a poet or not, to know the culture, history, tradition, and literature of both languages and countries.

The greatest rewards for me personally, both as a translator and a poet, were the bilingual readings where the poet read her original verses in Polish and I presented their English renditions. And to top it all, when the poet was my mother. The audiences, many of them bilingual, were thrilled to discover that the same poem could be comparably poetic and powerful in another language.

That's why, as the editor of the poetry translations section at *Loch Raven Review*, I have focused on bilingual publications. My goal is to familiarize readers with lesser-known poets from all over the world and with their translators, who work mostly for the love of poetry, poets and languages. Up to now I have presented poets writing in Spanish, Polish, Czech, Turkish, French, Portuguese, Mayan, Hebrew, Korean, Russian, and Vietnamese. The Translations Section in each issue is dedicated to one language, and features up to three different poets and their translators. Translation is indispensable in creating conversations between different cultures and nations and thus discovering a shared humanity, while at the same time it is its own artistic form.

Notes

"Dream in a Red Coat"
rogatywka cap: peaked, four-pointed cap used by various Polish military formations

"Lilac Lilacs"
"Lilac smells like...lilac." - inspired by Antoni Słonimski's poem, one of my favorites, "Żal" (Regret): "...a bez tak pachniał jak bez..." (and the lilac smelled like lilac...)

"Coffee with Carya"
Wigilia Supper, the traditional Christmas Eve vigil supper, held on December 24
Wio, wio: to urge horses to go
dwór: manor house; after WWII, the Communist government took over all estates

"Morelia: Dance of the Globes"
skwer: town square
Morelia: capital city of the Michoacán state in Mexico

"Holiday Morning in the Tatra Mountains"
Giewont: a mountain towering over the town of Zakopane. Legend has it that Giewont is a sleeping knight who will awake when the time comes.

"Before a Human Killed With a Human"
written on September 11, 2001

About the Authors

❖

Danuta E. Kosk-Kosicka is a biochemist, bilingual poet, writer, poetry translator, photographer, and co-editor of the literary journal *Loch Raven Review*. Her chapbook *Oblige the Light*, is the winner of the fifth annual Clarinda Harriss Poetry Prize (CityLit Press). Her poems have appeared in *A Narrow Fellow, Baltimore Review, Little Patuxent Review, Passager, Spillway,* and elsewhere. Her translations of Maryland Poets Laureate–Lucille Clifton, Josephine Jacobsen, and Linda Pastan– have been published in Poland. Her translations of Lidia Kosk, Ernest Bryll, and Wisława Szymborska's poems have appeared in the USA. She is also the translator for two bilingual books by Lidia Kosk: *niedosyt/reshapings* and *Słodka woda, słona woda/Sweet Water, Salt Water*. She resides in Baltimore County, MD.

Lidia Kosk is the author of eleven books of poetry and short stories, as well as two poetry and short fiction anthologies that she compiled and edited. She collaborated with her late husband, Henryk P. Kosk, on the two-volume *Poland's Generals: A Popular Biographical Lexicon*. Her poems have been published in *The Blue Lyra Review, The*

Fourth River, International Poetry Review, Interpoezia, Lalitamba, and elsewhere. Her poetry has been translated into eleven languages, and into choral compositions and multimedia video presentations. She was featured, with Danuta, on WYPR's (Baltimore's National Public Radio station) "The Signal." Lidia, a lawyer, humanitarian, and world traveler, resides in Warsaw, Poland, where she leads literary workshops and a Poets' Theater.

Apprentice House is the country's only campus-based, student-staffed book publishing company. Directed by professors and industry professionals, it is a nonprofit activity of the Communication Department at Loyola University Maryland.

Using state-of-the-art technology and an experiential learning model of education, Apprentice House publishes books in untraditional ways. This dual responsibility as publishers and educators creates an unprecedented collaborative environment among faculty and students, while teaching tomorrow's editors, designers, and marketers.

Outside of class, progress on book projects is carried forth by the AH Book Publishing Club, a co-curricular campus organization supported by Loyola University Maryland's Office of Student Activities.

Eclectic and provocative, Apprentice House titles intend to entertain as well as spark dialogue on a variety of topics. Financial contributions to sustain the press's work are welcomed. Contributions are tax deductible to the fullest extent allowed by the IRS.

To learn more about Apprentice House books or to obtain submission guidelines, please visit www.apprenticehouse.com.

Apprentice House
Communication Department
Loyola University Maryland
4501 N. Charles Street
Baltimore, MD 21210
Ph: 410-617-5265 • Fax: 410-617-2198
info@apprenticehouse.com • www.apprenticehouse.com

www.ingramcontent.com/pod-product-compliance
Lightning Source LLC
LaVergne TN
LVHW041207080426
835508LV00008B/849